www.finishinglinepress.com

first snow

poems by

Lynda McKinney Lambert

Finishing Line Press
Georgetown, Kentucky

first snow

ACKNOWLEDGMENTS

Grateful acknowledgment is made to the editors of the following journals
and anthologies in which these poems or earlier versions of them appeared:

Indiana Voice Journal~~"Pantoum to Winter"
Magnets & Ladders~~"Dream Sequence (1-7)," First published as "In my
    dream;" "My Daughter Cut the Roses;" "Silver Cloud Dancers"
Mingled Voices 2, Proverse Poetry Prize Anthology, Hong Kong, 2017~~"Red
    December"
Nature Writing~~"first snow;" "flamboyant;" "nature writes post cards;"
    "Partridge Breasted Aloe;" "we stand in darkness"
Plum Tree Tavern~~"crisp light at high noon;" "decades of winter winds;"
    "fanfare & ballyhoo;" "wintry nights"
Spent Blossoms~~"stony paths disappear" Edited by Claire Everett. Tanka
    Society of America Anthology, 2015.
The Weekly Avocet~~"aubergine morning;" "wintry morning"
Wordgathering~~"When we Dance Together"

Publisher: Leah Maines
Editor: Christen Kincaid
Cover Art: Lynda McKinney Lambert
Author Photo: Charles R. (Bob) Lambert
Cover Design: Elizabeth Maines McCleavy

Printed in the USA on acid-free paper.
Order online: www.finishinglinepress.com
    also available on amazon.com

Author inquiries and mail orders:
Finishing Line Press
P. O. Box 1626
Georgetown, Kentucky 40324
U. S. A.

Table of Contents

This collection of poems, first snow, *is dedicated to Dr. Ann Paton, a retired Professor of English from Geneva College, Beaver Falls, PA. Ann mentored and inspired me since I met her in 1996, when I arrived at Geneva College as a new professor.*

Authors Comment—May 2019

When my poem, 'first snow" was published in *NatureWriting Literary Magazine* on November 26, 2017, my desire to create a wintry-themed chapbook crystalized in my mind. Each poem is a snapshot-view or a glimpse of something that feels like a vision in a dream.

first snow, is a collection of thirty wintry-themed poetic snapshots that form a passage between the external world and the world within; a pilgrimage destination; a heartfelt and authentic place; the life-cycle of all that exists; an abode where body, mind and spirit synchronize with natural elements.

Poems arrive ready to begin.
Poets are only the transportation.

~from Humility by Mary Oliver

first snow

we watch
for the first
snowfall
wait for
silent passage
along the banks of
ancient creeks

dull morning light
conceals
gold-plated Gingko leaves
beneath
new-fallen snow

Dream Sequence (1-7)

#1
In my dream
I am standing on the mountain
near the terrifying precipice
sit down to draw in my sketchbook.
I see Alpine villages in the valley below—
a scattered helix of multi-colored
Tourmaline stones.

#2
In my dream
I am in death-defying situations
always in winter—I struggle
icy winds and dicey slopes
without a pathway.

#3
In my dream
my solo flights are joyous.
I push my heels downward
launch my body into the sky.
 Hover. Dive. Swoop. Circle.
No need for feathered wings.

#4
In my dream
I climb upwards
on the ladder I stumbled upon
in the woods one afternoon.
Earth disappears
the ladder is unstable
"Keep it straight up," I whisper.
"Keep your body centered. Stay poised."

#5
In my dream
I hold asymmetrical yellow wildflowers
planted by birds and wind in open fields.
A white dog guards the entrance to the Underworld.
She sleeps under my bed
protects me on long narrow journeys.

#6
In my dream
I rest in the shade of hemlocks and ferns,
gather water-worn grey stones
from shallow tributaries
glide on the surface of the river
beneath drooping Hemlock boughs
in my red canoe.

#7
In my dream
I watch movements as dusty stars
leave faint traces
on snow-covered path.

we stand in darkness

we stand in darkness
urging Blood Moon-arise
hover above the tree tops
slip past earth's shadows-
become a total eclipse

Pantoum to Winter

God viewed the transitory seasons
helped them change their clothes
painted the earth with vibrant strokes
sang at the birth of opalescent skies

helped them change their clothes
dressed the earth in sparkling white diamonds
sang at the birth of opalescent skies
hung frozen glass wind-chimes on snow laden trees

dressed the earth in sparkling white diamonds
stopped awhile to make snow angels in the windswept field
hung frozen glass wind-chimes on snow laden trees
called forth scarlet-feathered birds to brighten the pale slate sky

stopped awhile to make snow angels in the windswept field
painted the earth with vibrant strokes
called forth scarlet-feathered birds to brighten the pale slate sky
God viewed the transitory seasons.

January scene

dull morning light
blurs overview—
rows of worn-out mailboxes
rusted red, grey-green,
hoary weathered metal,
one newly painted
optimistic silver.

across the street
bare maple branches grasp curled-up
leaves trapped in wintry spines
a torn umbrella partly opened.

my body aches
moves slowly beneath
hand-stitched cotton quilt
where two lovers slept
entwined through-out
frigid January night.

sheltering pines in early fog
embrace neighboring homes
yellow house lurks
behind ancient blue spruce
nearly twice its height
burnt-orange abode broods
in the distance between
rows of naked maple trees.

wintry nights

wintry nights
frozen sugar maple branches
ensnared warp
curled russet leaves
weaving on a silvery weft

decades of bitter winds

decades of bitter winds
whipped and thrashed
flagellated and whisked
the row of red barberry bushes
grasping thorny spines
blown towards the west
search the twilight for
last rays of winter light
dangling crimson berries quiver

crisp light at high noon

crisp light at high noon
motionless blue spruce branches
soundless feathered wings

effervescent fog

effervescent fog
hovers over swift river
vaporized water
aquatic alterations
predict modifications

Leaving Köenigsee
A trip from Köenigsee, Germany to Grödig, Austria

Swift winds bring low temperatures
clouds conceal marble mountain peaks

Chiffon grey skies
press down on clustered red-tiled roofs
narrow doorways, slow moving tourists
leaving Köenigsee.

Our long ferry boat glides silently
across glacial-green Alpine lake
laughing Germans sing of home
frigid waves break around our boat.

In tonight's final hours
before snow-capped mountains
disappeared in the fog
my chilled body seeks shelter
I catch the next bus to Grödig.

nature writes post cards

nature writes post cards
on early morning sidewalks
across frozen stones
between layers of bronzed leaves
dripping from cold icicles

stony paths disappear

stony paths disappear
beneath my feet
I am the darkness
of gingko trees
and indigo skies

Silver Cloud Dancers

Silver clouds swirl & spin in circles
Inflated silence above her golden head. She
Levitates above the floor, reaches for
Variable visions of mesmerizing cloud-pillows.
Eternally drifting in uncertain lifecycles
Round & square. Touch the floating orbs.

Cloud dancer stretches her slender hands
Longevity is unpredictable, uncertain
Out-of-the-box survival fluctuates
Undulates
Determined by chemistry & chaos.

Dance your memories in silver clouds
Air and pure helium lift in rhythm
No one can calculate your journeys
Choreography of individual flights
Every Friday morning new clouds arrive
Repeat the process of new expectations
Some silver clouds last for a week. Some don't.

Boji

Boji holds
balance and heat
join
subtle sensations
with strongest vibrations
urges me—'Lay down!"
release energy blocks
Boji alchemy!
precious stones
healing, powerful
my hands blush like a crimson moon
seeds of ancient philosophers
planted metaphysical secrets
washed, purified by astral light
I feel clean—refreshed
pain is gone
Boji heals an aching heart
male and female
one crystal-centered male
smooth stones are always girls
males are scarce—expensive
heavier stones are always boys
showing off
yin & yang
negative & positive
magnetic attraction rock
my fingers tingle
my lips explore your surface
with a kiss.

Red December

New-fallen snow glimmers in pre-dawn darkness
shriveled red barberries dangle from thin bare branches
I shuffle my feet, dig in to feel solid ground
near the place where my Father's red roses
are surrounded by pillows of snow
slumbering safe in dark red December.

My heavy suede boots part the snow
It's too early for the red cardinals
"Where do they go at night?"
A sharp wind makes me huddle deeper
into my bright red boucle' jacket
while my two dogs search random trails
follow the long marks, meander downhill.

On a crisp day in mid-December
I desire red raspberry jam on warm toast
linger by the tall pampas grass
weighted down to the ground with icy snow
I think of strawberry Sundays with whipped cream
I recall wearing Neiman Marcus Red lipstick and
dancing all night in
hot red stilettos and tight blue jeans.

We turn around—for the return home
the dogs circle in the frozen pachysandra patches
stiff, malachite-green shrunken leaves.
In memories I see my neighbor walking to her car
she wears a cranberry red hat, worsted red wool coat, flat, scarlet red
    shoes
carries a true-red leather handbag like the one I bought last Sunday.

I watched her from the upstairs window.
In her 80s, she revealed how to live a gallant life.

No cars pass us on the country road this morning in red December
Where it is perpetual winter.

Partridge Breasted Aloe

She thrust her pointed daggers
upward and outward
concave deep green leaves
adorned with white spots
front and back.
Basks in winter sunshine
from a center core at the base
spiny and plump
with white designs
on the spruce green leaves.

Winter is flowering season
one long stem bursts above
like a quiet barn swallow
shooting up from the center
of a rosette in the springtime
one salmon pink flower
fills my mornings with a delicate scent
no fragrance can match
the fragile beauty of her perfume.

Partridge Breast is a sun worshipper
thrives in the south-facing window
prefers to drink less in winter.

Partridge Breast is the Queen of my collection
succulents and cacti, my delights.
Partridge Breasted Aloe brings
a sense of peace to my home.
When spring rains turn towards
Summer's cat-like days
my succulent friends spend their
vacation on my sun-drenched porch
where no grooming is necessary.

When We Dance Together

When we dance together in disguise
concealed behind black leather
dense fringes snap in the wind
 we spiral downward—a bizarre tale

Concealed behind black leather
hunker down against brisk mountain air
we spiral downward—a bizarre tale
wild rock-n-roll women in masquerade

Hunker down against brisk mountain air
the throbbing steel tank between my legs
wild rock-n-roll women in masquerade
neon surges through our veins

The throbbing steel tank between my legs
with the rumble of Cobra drags
neon surges through our veins
lean into the slant wind that blows us around

With the rumble of Cobra drags
we ride side by side, with stars in our eyes
lean into the slant wind that blows us around
raise the fist of my icy cold left hand

We ride side by side, with stars in our eyes
on the rough pavement of the dance floor
raise the fist of my icy cold left hand
reach out to catch the storm

On the rough pavement of the dance floor
laughing with the painful gusts of rain
reach out to catch the storm
dancing together in disguise.

aubergine morning

aubergine morning
deep multi-layered heavens
distant indigo-splashed hills
plum trees lined up side by side
memorable alliances

Zen garden helix

Zen garden helix
rain-washed granite stone spiral
spring transformation
yellow-green lemongrass tufts
 beside red Japanese tree

morning hour

A nippy breeze
wrapped around my bare feet
soft grey cashmere clouds
in the early morning hour.

My own reflection
slowly materialized-
exposed, naked
on a clear icy glass
surface.

Outside frozen windowpane
an icicle boundary
surrounded my view
of the aging Douglas Fir.

I turned for a closer look
through the silent porthole.

Quick movements
in the shadow revealed
one tiny ruffled sparrow
a solo performer
hunkered down, deep
on snow-clogged branches.

Inside, this room is a blizzard-
a scattering of words lingered-
waiting to be gathered onto a page
in a winter bouquet-written
in spite of the bitter cold.

It feels like we have been here
for a thousand years
in the early morning hour.

flamboyant

noisy red-winged blackbird
avian show-off—pay attention!
can't miss his flamboyant solos
performing on stage
atop swaying cattails in swamp
lined-up on grey telephone wires
along dusty rural roadsides

abundant red-winged songbird
bold yellow and red feathers
boastful emblems on his shoulders
coat-of-arms brooches on wings-
glistening black spinel majestic bird

his mate is more conservative
a shy woman in streaked brown feathers
does not dress to impress
doesn't care for grand-standing or glitz
he seeks to entertain the crowd
she calmly searches hidden brush
selects twigs for warp and weft
unobtrusively weaves her fancy nest
confident artist welcomes domestic solitude
conjures daydreams of spring
their eggs will hatch in three weeks

fanfare and ballyhoo

final snowfall
advises slow-moving changes
floating, spiraling, dancing
whispering progression
hardy wet quiescent branches
undressed false acacia
fast-growing tree
black locust takes
a long nap
in rural woodlands
anticipating sunshine
after final snowfall
soft warm rain, new growth
fragrant clusters swagger
spring blossoms flourish
white, pink or purple attire
welcome the new season of
fanfare and ballyhoo

My Daughter Cut the Roses

My daughter looked
at the bouquet of fresh roses
 noticed two of them were drooping.
"Let me show you how to trim the roses
so they stay fresh and strong." she said.
Her hands held the roses tenderly
One-by-one, trimmed off extra leaves
"These will make the water stink," she said.
She found scissors in the drawer
put the roses in a bowl of tepid water
held each stem under water
sliced them all, diagonally—
"As I cut the rose under the water,
little bubbles of air come to the surface.
Now, when the rose inhales
it will only breathe water into it,
 it won't fill up with air.
The living water inside the stems
gives longer life to each rose."
She carried the freshened flowers
In the tall glass vase
back to the center of the dining room table
darkest crimson buds, sunny yellow petals,
deep green fern leaves
and a frilly white carnation.

wintry morning

wintry morning
descending
spiraling
snowing
gentle
puffy
still
ice
be
*

Lynda **McKinney Lambert's** interdisciplinary interests led her to a career in teaching across disciplines in fine art and English literature. She retired from her position of professor of fine arts and humanities from Geneva College in 2008 due to profound sight loss. She suddenly lost most of her sight in 2007 due to Ischemic Optic Neuropathy. This unexpected change in her life opened the door for her to pursue her love of writing full-time. She works from her rural western Pennsylvania home in The Village of Wurtemburg.

Her first full-length book, *Concerti: Psalms for the Pilgrimage* (Kota Press, 2002) was published while she was teaching. The book is a journey she experienced over a number of years wile teaching during the summers in Salzburg, Austria.

Lambert's second book, *Walking by Inner Vision: Stories & Poems* (DLD Books, 2017) is a year-long journey through the seasons from January through December. Each of the twelve chapters begins with a poem that sets the stage for the non-fiction essays that follow.

Lynda's third book is *Star Signs: New & Selected Poems* (DLD Books, 2019), a collection of poems that span Lambert's career as a poet. Her first published poem appeared in 1989 when she was pursuing the BFA degree in painting. This was the beginning of her publications of poetry and non-fiction essays that continued as she went on to graduate school to pursue the MFA degree in Painting. After completing this degree, she completed the MA in English with her focus on poetry.

Lynda's themes are located in her love of nature, the rural landscape, dreams, mythology, fine art, and literature from antiquity to post-modernity.